From Startup to Success : Scaling Up , Tactics for Growing Your Business and Maximizing Success

Frederic BEHE

Chapter 1: Introduction to Scaling and Growth

As a business owner or entrepreneur, you likely have a vision for your company's future. Whether it's expanding into new markets, increasing revenue, or achieving greater market share, the key to realizing your vision is scaling and growth. However, scaling and growth can be challenging, and without the right strategies and resources, it can be difficult to achieve sustainable success.

In this chapter, we'll explore the importance of scaling and growth for businesses, the benefits and risks of pursuing growth, and different types of growth strategies. By understanding the basics of scaling and growth, you'll be better equipped to develop a roadmap for achieving your business goals and maximizing your potential for success.

We'll start by examining why scaling and growth are crucial for businesses of all sizes, and the advantages they offer in terms of market share, profitability, and innovation. We'll also discuss the potential risks and challenges associated with growth, such as increased competition, financial risks, and organizational complexity. By understanding both the benefits and risks of growth, you'll be able to make informed decisions about how to approach scaling your business.

Next, we'll dive into different types of growth strategies, such as market penetration, market development, product development, and diversification. We'll examine the advantages and disadvantages of each strategy, and how to choose the right approach for your business. By developing a clear growth strategy, you'll be able to focus your resources and efforts on the most effective areas of growth.

This chapter will provide a solid foundation for understanding the importance of scaling and growth for businesses, as well as the key strategies and considerations for pursuing growth effectively. Whether you're a startup founder or a seasoned business owner, this chapter will help you start thinking strategically about how to take your business to the next level.

1.1 Why scaling and growth are important for businesses

While scaling and growth can offer many benefits for businesses, they also come with significant challenges and risks that need to be carefully managed.

Here are some of the most common challenges and risks associated with scaling and growth:

Increased complexity:

As your business grows, it becomes more complex to manage. You may need to develop new processes and systems to manage increased sales, larger teams, and more complex operations. This can lead to organizational silos, communication breakdowns, and decreased efficiency.

Financial risks:

Scaling and growth require significant investment, which can put a strain on your finances. You may need to secure additional funding through loans, investors, or other sources, which can come with increased debt and interest payments. Additionally, there is a risk that your investment in growth may not pay off in the long run, leading to financial losses.

Increased competition:

As you grow, you'll likely face increased competition from both established players in your industry and new startups. This can lead to price pressure, decreased market share, and decreased profitability.
Talent management: As you grow, you'll need to attract, retain, and manage a larger team of employees. This can be challenging, particularly if you're trying to maintain a strong company culture and attract top talent in a competitive market.

Operational challenges:

Scaling and growth can also lead to operational challenges, such as inventory management, logistics, and supply chain management. These challenges can become more complex and difficult to manage as your business grows.

Regulatory and legal challenges:

Finally, scaling and growth can also lead to regulatory and legal challenges, particularly if you're expanding into new markets or launching new products or services. You may need to navigate complex regulatory frameworks and comply with new laws and regulations, which can be time-consuming and expensive.

It's important to be aware of the challenges and risks associated with scaling and growth, and to develop strategies to manage them effectively. By carefully planning your growth strategy, investing in the right resources and systems, and staying agile in the face of change, you can position your business for sustainable success in the long term.

1.2 The challenges and risks of scaling and growth

Cultural challenges:

As your business grows, it can become more difficult to maintain the same level of company culture and values that made you successful in the first place. You'll need to work to ensure that your culture remains strong and that your employees remain engaged and motivated, even as your business expands.

Supply chain disruptions:

Scaling and growth can also lead to disruptions in your supply chain, particularly if you're sourcing materials or products from new suppliers. It's important to carefully vet your suppliers and build redundancies into your supply chain to minimize the risk of disruptions.

Technology challenges:

As you grow, you may need to invest in new technology systems to manage your operations and support your growth. This can be costly and time-consuming, and there is a risk that your new systems may not be fully integrated with your existing systems or may not meet your needs in the long term.

Market shifts:

Finally, it's important to be aware of the risk of market shifts and changes in consumer behavior. Just because your business is successful now doesn't mean it will be successful in the future, particularly if your industry is disrupted by new technologies or changing consumer preferences. It's important to stay agile and adaptable in the face of change, and to be prepared to pivot your strategy as needed to stay ahead of the competition.

Scaling and growth can be incredibly rewarding, but they also come with significant challenges and risks that need to be carefully managed. By being aware of these challenges and developing strategies to mitigate them, you can position your business for sustainable success in the long term.

1.3 The benefits of scaling and growth

While scaling and growth come with significant challenges and risks, they also offer many benefits for businesses.

Here are some of the most common benefits of scaling and growth:

Increased revenue and profitability:

One of the most obvious benefits of scaling and growth is increased revenue and profitability. As you expand into new markets and increase your sales volume, you'll be able to generate more revenue and increase your profit margins.

Greater market share:

Scaling and growth can also help you capture a greater share of the market in your industry. This can help you establish yourself as a leader in your field and make it more difficult for competitors to gain a foothold in your market.

Economies of scale:

As you scale and grow your business, you may be able to achieve economies of scale, which can help you reduce your costs and increase your efficiency. For example, you may be able to negotiate better prices with suppliers, reduce your overhead costs by spreading them over a larger revenue base, or streamline your operations by investing in new technology or systems.

Increased brand recognition:

As you expand into new markets and increase your sales volume, you'll also increase your brand recognition and awareness. This can help you attract new customers and increase your customer loyalty, as well as make it easier to attract top talent to your team.

Diversification:

Scaling and growth can also help you diversify your revenue streams and reduce your dependence on any one market or product. This can help you weather economic downturns or changes in consumer behavior, and make your business more resilient in the long term.

Opportunities for innovation:

Finally, scaling and growth can provide new opportunities for innovation and creativity within your business. As you expand into new markets and explore new products or services, you may discover new ways to innovate and differentiate yourself from your competitors.

While scaling and growth come with significant challenges and risks, they also offer many potential benefits for businesses. By carefully managing the risks and investing in the resources and systems needed to support your growth, you can position your business for sustainable success in the long term.

1.4 Different types of growth strategies

Market penetration:

This strategy involves focusing on increasing your market share in your existing market. You may do this by offering promotions, increasing your advertising and marketing efforts, or offering new product lines to your existing customer base. The goal is to gain a larger share of your current market and increase revenue.

Market development:

This strategy involves expanding into new markets with your existing products or services. This can involve targeting new demographics or geographic regions, or exploring new distribution channels. The goal is to increase revenue by tapping into new markets without developing new products or services.

Product development:

This strategy involves developing new products or services to offer to your existing customers. This can involve creating new variations of your existing products, or developing entirely new products or services that complement your existing offerings. The goal is to increase revenue by offering more options to your existing customer base.

Diversification:

This strategy involves expanding into new markets or developing new products or services that are unrelated to your existing offerings. This can involve expanding into new industries or leveraging your existing capabilities to develop new products or services. The goal is to reduce your dependence on any one market or product and create new revenue streams.

Merger or acquisition:

This strategy involves acquiring or merging with another company to increase your market share or gain access to new capabilities or resources. This can help you expand into new markets or increase your competitive advantage in your existing market. The goal is to create synergies that result in increased revenue and profitability.

Franchising:

This strategy involves expanding your business by allowing other entrepreneurs to operate their own franchises under your brand. This can help you expand into new geographic regions or industries without the need for significant capital investment. The goal is to increase revenue by leveraging the resources and capabilities of your franchisees.

There are many different types of growth strategies that businesses can pursue. The key is to carefully evaluate your options and choose the strategy that best aligns with your business goals and resources.

Chapter 2: Assessing Your Business's Readiness for Growth

Scaling and growing your business can be an exciting prospect, but it's important to ensure that your business is truly ready for the next level of growth. Before embarking on any growth strategies, it's critical to take a step back and evaluate your business's readiness for growth.

In this chapter, we'll explore the key factors that you should consider when assessing your business's readiness for growth. We'll discuss the importance of having a strong foundation in place, including a solid business plan, robust financial systems, and a talented team. We'll also explore the importance of having a growth mindset and a willingness to take calculated risks.

By the end of this chapter, you'll have a clear understanding of the key factors that contribute to a business's readiness for growth, and you'll be better equipped to evaluate your own business's strengths and weaknesses. This will help you make informed decisions about the types of growth strategies that are most appropriate for your business and ensure that you're well-positioned for long-term success.

2.1 Understanding your current business model and its limitations

Before embarking on any growth strategies, it's important to have a clear understanding of your current business model and its limitations. This includes understanding your target market, the value you provide to customers, and the resources you have available to deliver that value.

Assessing your current business model can help you identify areas of strength as well as areas that may need improvement in order to support growth. For example, you may need to refine your value proposition, explore new distribution channels, or invest in additional resources in order to scale your business.

It's also important to understand the limitations of your current business model. This includes understanding any operational constraints, market limitations, or competitive pressures that may make it difficult to grow your business. For example, you may be operating in a highly saturated market with limited opportunities for growth, or you may be facing regulatory or legal hurdles that limit your ability to expand into new markets.

By understanding your current business model and its limitations, you can identify the areas where you need to focus your efforts in order to successfully scale your business. This may involve making changes to your existing business model or exploring new models that better align with your growth objectives.

Understanding your current business model and its limitations is a critical first step in assessing your business's readiness for growth. By taking the time to carefully evaluate your current situation, you can identify the areas that require improvement and develop a clear roadmap for achieving your growth objectives.

2.2 Evaluating your resources and capabilities

In order to successfully scale your business, you need to have the resources and capabilities necessary to support growth. This includes having the right people, technology, and infrastructure in place to deliver on your growth objectives.

When evaluating your resources and capabilities, it's important to consider both your current capacity and your future needs. This includes assessing your current workforce and identifying any skills gaps that may need to be filled in order to support growth. You'll also need to evaluate your technology infrastructure and ensure that it can scale to meet your future needs.

You should evaluate your financial resources and ensure that you have sufficient capital to support growth. This may involve seeking additional funding, optimizing your cash flow, or reducing unnecessary expenses.

It's also important to consider your intangible resources and capabilities, such as your brand reputation, customer relationships, and intellectual property. These intangible assets can be a valuable source of competitive advantage and may play a critical role in supporting your growth objectives.

By evaluating your resources and capabilities, you can identify the areas where you may need to invest in order to support growth. This may involve hiring additional staff, upgrading your technology, or developing new intellectual property. By proactively addressing these needs, you can ensure that you're well-positioned to achieve your growth objectives and capitalize on new opportunities as they arise.

Assessing your resources and capabilities is a critical step in evaluating your business's readiness for growth. By understanding your strengths and weaknesses in these areas, you can develop a clear roadmap for achieving your growth objectives and ensuring long-term success.

2.3 Identifying potential growth opportunities

In order to scale your business, it's important to identify potential growth opportunities. This may involve expanding your product or service offerings, entering new markets, or exploring new distribution channels.

One way to identify potential growth opportunities is to conduct market research and analyze industry trends. This can help you identify emerging markets, changing customer needs, and new technologies that may create new opportunities for growth.

You should also consider the competitive landscape and identify areas where you may be able to gain a competitive advantage. This may involve developing new intellectual property, optimizing your supply chain, or partnering with other companies to leverage their expertise.

Another important consideration when identifying potential growth opportunities is your own strengths and capabilities. This includes your existing customer base, your brand reputation, and your unique value proposition. By leveraging these strengths, you may be able to identify new opportunities that are well-aligned with your existing business model.

Identifying potential growth opportunities requires a deep understanding of your industry, your customers, and your own strengths and weaknesses. By taking a strategic approach to identifying new opportunities, you can ensure that you're well-positioned to capitalize on emerging trends and achieve your growth objectives.

2.4 Analyzing market trends and competition

To assess your business's readiness for growth, it's important to analyze market trends and competition. This involves conducting a thorough analysis of your industry, including the size of the market, key players, and emerging trends.

Market research can help you identify potential opportunities for growth, as well as areas of the market that may be oversaturated or in decline. It can also help you understand the needs and preferences of your target customers, which can inform your growth strategy.

Analyzing your competition is also an important part of assessing your business's readiness for growth. This involves understanding your competitors' strengths and weaknesses, as well as their strategies for growth. This can help you identify areas where you may be able to gain a competitive advantage and develop a strategy that differentiates you from the competition.

To analyze market trends and competition, you may use a variety of research methods, including surveys, focus groups, and secondary research sources such as industry reports and news articles. You may also use tools like SWOT analysis (Strengths, Weaknesses, Opportunities, Threats) to help you identify areas where you can leverage your strengths and mitigate potential risks.

Analyzing market trends and competition is a critical step in assessing your business's readiness for growth. By understanding your industry and competitors, you can identify potential growth opportunities and develop a strategy that positions you for long-term success.

Chapter 3: Developing a Growth Strategy

Assessing your business's readiness for growth is an important first step in the scaling process. Once you've identified potential growth opportunities and analyzed the market and competition, the next step is to develop a growth strategy that aligns with your business goals and objectives.

In this chapter, we'll explore the key steps involved in developing a growth strategy. This includes identifying your growth goals, assessing your strengths and weaknesses, and developing a plan to achieve your objectives.

We'll also discuss the importance of aligning your growth strategy with your business model, as well as the importance of ongoing monitoring and evaluation to ensure that your strategy remains effective in the long term.

Whether you're looking to expand your product offerings, enter new markets, or scale your operations, developing a growth strategy is an essential part of the process. By taking a strategic approach to growth, you can position your business for long-term success and achieve your goals in a sustainable and scalable way.

3.1 Setting goals and objectives

When developing a growth strategy, it's important to start by setting clear and measurable goals and objectives. This involves identifying the specific outcomes you want to achieve through your growth efforts, such as increasing revenue, expanding your customer base, or entering new markets.

Setting goals and objectives can help you stay focused and aligned as you develop and execute your growth strategy. It also enables you to track progress and measure success over time.

To set effective goals and objectives, it's important to make sure they are:

- Specific: Clearly define what you want to achieve and why it matters for your business.

- Measurable: Establish metrics that will enable you to track progress and measure success.

- Achievable: Ensure that your goals and objectives are realistic and attainable given your current resources and capabilities.

- Relevant: Ensure that your goals and objectives are aligned with your overall business strategy and long-term objectives.

- Time-bound: Set a specific timeframe for achieving your goals and objectives.

By setting clear and measurable goals and objectives, you can ensure that your growth strategy is focused, aligned, and effective. This can help you achieve your desired outcomes in a sustainable and scalable way, positioning your business for long-term success.

3.2 Choosing the right growth strategy for your business

Once you've set clear and measurable goals and objectives, the next step is to choose the right growth strategy for your business. There are several different growth strategies that businesses can pursue, depending on their goals, resources, and market conditions.
Some common growth strategies include:

Market penetration:

Market penetration is a growth strategy that involves focusing on increasing market share in your existing market by selling more of your current products or services. This can involve increasing sales to current customers, as well as attracting new customers within your existing market.

There are several ways to pursue market penetration, including:

- Pricing: Adjusting your pricing strategy to make your products or services more competitive and attractive to customers.

- Promotion: Increasing your marketing and advertising efforts to increase awareness of your products or services.

- Product improvements: Making improvements or updates to your existing products or services to make them more desirable to customers.

- Distribution channels: Expanding your distribution channels to make it easier for customers to purchase your products or services.

The benefits of pursuing a market penetration strategy include:

- Increased market share: By selling more of your existing products or services, you can increase your market share and strengthen your position in your existing market.

- Increased revenue: As you sell more products or services, your revenue will increase, which can help fund further growth efforts.

- Improved brand recognition: By increasing your presence in your existing market, you can improve brand recognition and awareness among customers.

It's important to consider the potential risks and challenges associated with a market penetration strategy, such as increased competition and potential price wars. It's important to carefully assess the market conditions and competition before pursuing a market penetration strategy, and to make sure you have the resources and capabilities to effectively execute the strategy.

Product development:

Product development is a growth strategy that involves developing new products or services to sell to your existing customers. This can involve improving or updating your current offerings, as well as introducing completely new products or services.

There are several benefits of pursuing a product development strategy, including:

- Diversification of revenue streams: By introducing new products or services, you can diversify your revenue streams and reduce your reliance on any one product or service.

- Increased customer loyalty: By offering new and improved products or services, you can increase customer loyalty and retention.

- Improved brand recognition: Introducing new products or services can help improve brand recognition and awareness among customers.

When pursuing a product development strategy, it's important to consider factors such as market demand, customer needs, and competition. It's also important to have the resources and capabilities to effectively develop and market new products or services.

There are several ways to approach product development, including:

- Improving existing products or services: Making improvements or updates to your current offerings to make them more desirable to customers.

- Introducing new products or services: Developing completely new products or services that are complementary to your existing offerings or that address unmet customer needs.

- Partnering or acquiring other companies: Partnering with or acquiring other companies that have complementary products or services that can be integrated into your offerings.

It's important to carefully assess the market conditions and competition before pursuing a product development strategy, and to make sure you have the resources and capabilities to effectively execute the strategy.

Market development:

Market development is a growth strategy that involves expanding into new markets with your existing products or services. This can involve targeting new customer segments, geographic regions, or distribution channels.

There are several benefits of pursuing a market development strategy, including:

- Increased customer base: By expanding into new markets, you can increase your customer base and revenue potential.

- Diversification of revenue streams: By targeting new markets, you can diversify your revenue streams and reduce your reliance on any one market.

- Improved brand recognition: Expanding into new markets can help improve brand recognition and awareness among customers.

When pursuing a market development strategy, it's important to consider factors such as market size, competition, and customer needs. It's also important to have the resources and capabilities to effectively market and sell your products or services in the new market.

There are several ways to approach market development, including:

- Geographic expansion: Expanding into new geographic regions where there is demand for your products or services.

- Targeting new customer segments: Identifying new customer segments that could benefit from your products or services.

- New distribution channels: Identifying new distribution channels to sell your products or services, such as online marketplaces or retail partnerships.

It's important to carefully assess the market conditions and competition before pursuing a market development strategy, and to make sure you have the resources and capabilities to effectively execute the strategy.

Diversification:

Diversification is a growth strategy that involves expanding your business into new products, services, or markets that are different from your current offerings. This can involve either related or unrelated diversification.

Related diversification involves expanding into products, services, or markets that are related to your existing business. This can involve leveraging existing capabilities, resources, and brand recognition to enter new markets or develop new products or services.

Unrelated diversification, on the other hand, involves expanding into completely new and unrelated products, services, or markets. This can involve entering industries or markets that are completely different from your existing business, and often requires a significant investment of time and resources.

There are several benefits of pursuing a diversification strategy, including:

- Risk reduction: By diversifying your business into new products, services, or markets, you can reduce your reliance on any one product, service, or market, and reduce your overall business risk.

- Increased revenue potential: By entering new markets or developing new products or services, you can increase your revenue potential and tap into new customer segments.

- Competitive advantage: By diversifying your business, you can develop new capabilities, resources, and expertise that give you a competitive advantage over rivals.

When pursuing a diversification strategy, it's important to carefully assess the potential risks and rewards, and to ensure that you have the resources and capabilities to effectively execute the strategy. This may involve developing new capabilities, hiring new talent, or partnering with other companies to fill any gaps in your expertise or resources.

Diversification can be a powerful growth strategy, but it's important to approach it carefully and with a clear understanding of the potential risks and rewards.

When choosing the right growth strategy for your business, it's important to consider factors such as your current market position, resources and capabilities, and competitive landscape. It's also important to consider the potential risks and challenges associated with each strategy, as well as the potential rewards and opportunities.

By choosing the right growth strategy for your business, you can position yourself for long-term success and achieve your growth goals in a sustainable and scalable way.

3.3 Creating a roadmap for growth

Once you have chosen a growth strategy for your business, it's important to create a roadmap that outlines the specific steps and milestones needed to achieve your growth goals. This roadmap should be a comprehensive plan that covers all aspects of your business, including marketing, sales, operations, and finance.

Here are some key steps to consider when creating a roadmap for growth:

Define your growth goals:

Defining your growth goals is a critical first step in creating a roadmap for growth. Your growth goals should be specific, measurable, achievable, relevant, and time-bound (SMART).

Here are some tips for defining your growth goals:

- Be specific: Your growth goals should be specific and clearly defined. For example, instead of setting a goal to "increase sales," you may set a goal to "increase sales by 25% within the next 12 months. »

- Make them measurable: Your growth goals should be measurable so that you can track progress and determine whether you have achieved them. This may involve setting specific targets for revenue, market share, or other key performance metrics.

- Ensure they are achievable: Your growth goals should be realistic and achievable based on your current resources, capabilities, and market conditions. While it's important to set ambitious goals, it's also important to ensure that they are achievable given your current circumstances.

- Ensure they are relevant: Your growth goals should be relevant to your overall business strategy and aligned with your vision for the future of your business. This may involve identifying key market trends and opportunities that are relevant to your business, or setting goals that align with your mission and values.

- Make them time-bound: Your growth goals should be time-bound so that you have a clear deadline for achieving them. This may involve setting short-term, medium-term, and long-term goals that align with your overall growth strategy.

By defining specific, measurable, achievable, relevant, and time-bound growth goals, you can ensure that you have a clear direction for your growth strategy and a way to measure progress along the way.

This can help you stay focused and motivated as you work towards achieving your growth goals.

Identify key initiatives:

After defining your growth goals, the next step is to identify the key initiatives that will help you achieve those goals. Key initiatives are specific actions or projects that you will undertake to drive growth and achieve your goals.

Here are some tips for identifying key initiatives:

Prioritize your goals:

Start by prioritizing your growth goals based on their importance and potential impact on your business. This will help you focus on the most critical areas for growth.

Brainstorm potential initiatives:

Once you have identified your top growth goals, brainstorm potential initiatives that will help you achieve those goals. This may involve looking at successful growth strategies used by other businesses in your industry, or identifying new and innovative approaches to driving growth.

Evaluate feasibility and resources:

Evaluate the feasibility of each potential initiative based on your available resources, capabilities, and timeline. Determine which initiatives are realistic and achievable based on your current circumstances.

Create a roadmap:

Once you have identified your key initiatives, create a roadmap that outlines the specific actions, timelines, and resources required to achieve each initiative. This will help you stay organized and focused as you work towards achieving your growth goals.

Monitor progress:

Finally, monitor your progress on a regular basis and adjust your initiatives as needed based on your results. This will help you stay on track and ensure that you are making progress towards your growth goals.

By identifying key initiatives that are aligned with your growth goals, you can develop a clear plan for driving growth and achieving success in your business. This can help you stay focused, motivated, and on track as you work towards achieving your growth objectives.

Develop an action plan:

Developing an action plan is a critical step in creating a roadmap for growth. An action plan is a detailed outline of the steps that you will take to achieve your growth goals and implement your key initiatives.

Here are some steps to help you develop an effective action plan:

Break down your initiatives into specific actions:

For each key initiative, break down the specific actions that you will need to take to achieve your goals. These actions should be concrete and measurable, and should be directly linked to your overall growth objectives.

Assign responsibilities:

Identify who will be responsible for each action item, and assign clear roles and responsibilities to team members or stakeholders. This will help ensure that everyone knows what they need to do, and that progress is tracked and monitored effectively.

Set deadlines:

Establish realistic timelines for each action item, and set deadlines for completion. This will help ensure that everyone stays on track and that progress is made towards your growth goals.

Identify required resources:

Determine what resources will be needed to implement each action item, such as technology, funding, or staffing. This will help ensure that you have the necessary resources in place to achieve your growth objectives.

Monitor and adjust:

Regularly monitor progress against your action plan, and adjust as needed to ensure that you are on track to achieve your growth goals. This may involve modifying timelines, adjusting resource allocations, or redefining action items as new information becomes available.

By developing a detailed action plan, you can ensure that your growth initiatives are executed effectively and efficiently, and that you are making steady progress towards achieving your overall growth objectives.

Assign responsibilities:

When assigning responsibilities for your growth initiatives, it's important to clearly define each team member's role and ensure that everyone understands their responsibilities.

Here are some steps to help you effectively assign responsibilities:

Identify the skills and expertise needed:

Consider the skills and expertise required to successfully execute each initiative. This may include technical skills, project management expertise, or subject matter knowledge. Look for team members who have the necessary skills and experience to effectively execute each initiative.

Define clear roles and responsibilities:

Clearly define each team member's role and responsibilities. Be specific about what is expected of each person, and how their contributions will support the overall success of the initiative.

Establish clear communication channels:

Set up clear communication channels between team members and stakeholders to ensure that everyone is informed and up-to-date on progress. This can include regular check-ins, progress reports, or project management software.

Provide adequate training and support:

Ensure that team members have the necessary training and support to effectively execute their responsibilities. This may involve providing additional training, coaching, or mentoring to help team members build the skills and knowledge needed to succeed.

Establish accountability:

Establish clear accountability for each team member's responsibilities, and set up mechanisms to track progress and hold team members accountable for meeting their goals. This can include regular progress reviews, performance evaluations, or other measures to ensure that everyone is contributing effectively to the initiative.

By taking the time to effectively assign responsibilities, you can ensure that each team member is clear on their role and responsibilities, and that everyone is working together effectively towards achieving your growth objectives.

Monitor progress:

Monitoring progress is a critical part of executing a growth plan.

Here are some steps you can take to effectively monitor progress:

Establish clear performance metrics:

Define the key performance indicators (KPIs) that you will use to measure progress towards your growth goals. These metrics should be specific, measurable, and tied to your overall growth objectives.

Set up a regular review schedule:

Establish a regular review schedule to track progress against your KPIs. This can be daily, weekly, or monthly depending on the nature of the initiative and the timeline for achieving your growth objectives.

Use project management tools:

Use project management software or other tools to track progress and ensure that all team members are aligned on the status of each initiative. This can help identify any issues or roadblocks that may be impacting progress, and ensure that everyone is working towards the same goals.

Hold regular check-ins:

Schedule regular check-ins with team members to discuss progress, identify any issues, and ensure that everyone is aligned on next steps. This can be an opportunity to provide feedback, identify areas for improvement, and ensure that everyone is on track to meet their objectives.

Adjust your strategy as needed:

Based on your progress review, you may need to adjust your growth strategy or modify your approach to certain initiatives. This may involve changing your KPIs, adjusting timelines, or reallocating resources to address any issues or challenges that arise.

By monitoring progress on a regular basis, you can stay on top of any issues or challenges that may arise, and ensure that you are making progress towards your growth goals. This can help you stay focused on your objectives, make informed decisions, and ultimately achieve the growth and success that you are aiming for.

By creating a comprehensive roadmap for growth, you can ensure that everyone in your organization is aligned around your growth goals, and that you have a clear plan in place to achieve those goals. This can help you stay focused and on track as you navigate the challenges and opportunities of scaling and growth.

3.4 Measuring and tracking progress

Measuring and tracking progress is an essential aspect of implementing a growth strategy. It involves monitoring the performance of your business and evaluating whether you are making progress towards your growth goals. Here are some steps to consider when measuring and tracking progress:

Define your metrics:

Identify the key metrics that you will use to measure progress towards your growth objectives. These could include revenue growth, customer acquisition, market share, or other performance indicators that are relevant to your business.

Set targets:

Establish targets for each metric, based on your growth goals and your analysis of your business model and resources. These targets should be specific, measurable, and time-bound, and should align with your overall growth strategy.

Track performance:

Use software tools or other systems to track performance against your metrics and targets. This will help you identify trends, track progress over time, and identify areas where you may need to adjust your strategy or approach.

Analyze results:

Regularly analyze your performance data to identify areas where you are making progress and areas where you may need to make adjustments. This could involve analyzing trends, comparing your results to industry benchmarks, or conducting other types of analysis to gain insight into your business performance.

Adjust your strategy:

Based on your analysis of performance data, you may need to adjust your growth strategy or modify your approach to certain initiatives. This may involve changing your metrics, adjusting targets, or reallocating resources to address any issues or challenges that arise.

By measuring and tracking progress on a regular basis, you can stay on top of your business performance and make informed decisions about your growth strategy. This can help you identify areas of strength and weakness, focus your resources on initiatives that are driving growth, and ultimately achieve your growth objectives.

Chapter 4: Scaling Your Operations

Chapter 4 focuses on the critical process of scaling your operations, which involves expanding your capacity to meet the growing demands of your business. Scaling operations can be a complex and challenging process, but it is essential for businesses that want to achieve sustained growth over time. In this chapter, we will explore the key strategies and best practices for scaling operations effectively, including optimizing processes, leveraging technology, and developing a scalable workforce. By implementing these strategies, you can position your business to achieve greater efficiency, productivity, and profitability as you scale your operations to meet the needs of a growing customer base.

4.1 Streamlining processes and workflows

Streamlining processes and workflows is a crucial aspect of scaling operations. As your business grows, it's essential to optimize your processes and workflows to ensure that they are efficient, effective, and scalable. Streamlining processes and workflows can help you reduce waste, minimize errors, and increase productivity, which are all critical factors in achieving sustainable growth.

To streamline your processes and workflows, start by mapping out your current processes and identifying any bottlenecks or inefficiencies. Look for opportunities to automate repetitive tasks or eliminate unnecessary steps in the process. You can also consider adopting Lean or Six Sigma methodologies, which focus on continuous improvement and waste reduction.

Another effective strategy for streamlining processes and workflows is to implement technology solutions such as workflow automation software, project management tools, or customer relationship management (CRM) systems. These tools can help you automate routine tasks, track progress, and improve communication and collaboration among team members.

Streamlining processes and workflows is a critical step in scaling your operations. By optimizing your processes and workflows, you can improve efficiency, reduce costs, and position your business for sustainable growth.

4.2 Automating tasks and functions

Automation is a key strategy for scaling your operations, as it can help you save time, reduce costs, and improve accuracy. By automating tasks and functions, you can free up resources to focus on higher-value activities and improve overall efficiency.

One area where automation can be particularly beneficial is in repetitive or routine tasks. For example, you can automate data entry, invoicing, or order processing to reduce the workload on your team and minimize the risk of errors. You can also automate marketing campaigns, social media posts, or customer service responses to improve the customer experience and increase engagement.

Another area where automation can be useful is in data analysis and reporting. By automating data collection and analysis, you can gain valuable insights into your business operations, such as trends in customer behavior, sales performance, or inventory levels. These insights can help you make informed decisions about how to allocate resources and optimize your operations for growth.

When implementing automation, it's important to choose the right tools and technologies for your business. Look for solutions that are easy to use, integrate well with your existing systems, and offer robust features and functionality. You should also ensure that your team members are trained on how to use the automation tools effectively, and that you have appropriate safeguards in place to prevent errors or data breaches.

Automation can be a powerful tool for scaling your operations. By automating tasks and functions, you can improve efficiency, reduce costs, and position your business for sustained growth over time.

4.3 Outsourcing and delegating responsibilities

Outsourcing and delegating responsibilities are effective strategies for scaling your operations, especially when you have limited resources or expertise in-house. Outsourcing involves hiring external firms or contractors to handle specific tasks or functions, while delegating involves assigning responsibilities to your team members or departments.

Outsourcing can be particularly useful for non-core functions or specialized tasks that require specific expertise. For example, you may choose to outsource your accounting, legal, or IT support to external firms that have the necessary skills and experience. By outsourcing, you can reduce your workload, save time and resources, and gain access to specialized knowledge and technology.

Delegating responsibilities to your team members can also be an effective way to scale your operations. By empowering your team members to take on more responsibilities, you can improve productivity, creativity, and engagement, and free up your own time to focus on strategic initiatives. You can delegate responsibilities based on each team member's strengths and skills, and provide them with the necessary training and support to succeed in their new roles.

Outsourcing and delegating also come with potential risks and challenges. For example, outsourcing can lead to quality control issues or communication problems if you don't choose the right vendors or set clear expectations. Delegating can also be challenging if your team members don't have the necessary skills or experience, or if you don't provide them with clear guidelines and expectations.

To minimize these risks, it's important to choose outsourcing vendors or team members carefully, and to establish clear communication channels, expectations, and metrics for success. You should also monitor and evaluate the quality and effectiveness of outsourced or delegated tasks, and be prepared to make adjustments as needed.

Outsourcing and delegating can be effective strategies for scaling your operations and maximizing your resources. By choosing the right partners or team members and providing them with the necessary support and guidance, you can position your business for sustained growth and success.

4.4 Managing resources effectively

Managing resources effectively is crucial to successfully scale your operations. Here are some key areas to focus on:

Human resources:

As your business grows, you will need to hire more employees and possibly expand your management team. It's important to have clear job descriptions, performance metrics, and a solid hiring process in place to ensure that you're bringing on the right people for your team. Additionally, you'll want to consider employee development and training programs to help your team members grow and thrive in their roles.

Financial resources:

Scaling your operations will require a significant investment of capital. You'll need to ensure that you have enough cash flow and access to financing to support your growth plans. You should also establish financial controls and reporting systems to help you monitor your financial performance and make informed decisions.

Physical resources:

Depending on your business, scaling your operations may require investing in new equipment, technology, or facilities. You'll want to carefully evaluate your current assets and determine what additional resources you'll need to support your growth plans.

Time resources:

Scaling your operations can be time-consuming, and it's important to have a realistic understanding of the time commitment required to achieve your growth goals. This may involve delegating tasks, prioritizing projects, and finding ways to streamline your workflow to maximize efficiency.

Effective resource management requires careful planning, strong leadership, and a focus on continuous improvement. By investing in your resources and managing them effectively, you can position your business for sustainable growth and long-term success.

Chapter 5: Expanding into New Markets

Chapter 5 is all about expanding your business into new markets. This can include entering new geographical regions, targeting new customer demographics, or even developing new product lines. Expanding into new markets can be a key driver of growth for businesses, but it can also be a complex and challenging process. In this chapter, we will explore the various strategies and tactics that businesses can use to successfully expand into new markets. We will cover topics such as market research, customer segmentation, product development, and marketing strategies. Whether you are a small business looking to enter a new market or a large corporation seeking to diversify your offerings, this chapter will provide valuable insights and practical advice for achieving success in your expansion efforts.

5.1 Identifying new markets and opportunities

Identifying new markets and opportunities is the first step in expanding into new markets. Before you can enter a new market, you need to identify potential opportunities and determine if they align with your overall business strategy and goals.

Here are some key considerations when identifying new markets and opportunities:

Market Research:

Conduct market research to gain a better understanding of the new market you are considering. This research should include analysis of the market size, growth potential, competition, regulatory environment, and customer needs.

Customer Segmentation:

Identify the different customer segments within the new market and evaluate their needs, preferences, and buying habits. This will help you tailor your product or service offerings to better meet the needs of these customers.

Product Development:

Evaluate whether your current products or services are a good fit for the new market or if you need to develop new products or services that better align with the needs of the customers in the new market.

Partnering and Networking:

Identify potential partners, suppliers, and distributors in the new market who can help you navigate local regulations, customs, and cultural differences.

SWOT Analysis:

Conduct a SWOT analysis to evaluate your strengths, weaknesses, opportunities, and threats in the new market. This analysis can help you identify potential risks and challenges that you may face and develop strategies to address them.

By considering these factors, you can identify new markets and opportunities that are a good fit for your business and develop a plan to successfully enter and compete in those markets.

5.2 Conducting market research and analysis

Before expanding into new markets, it's important to conduct thorough market research and analysis to identify the most promising opportunities and ensure that you're making informed decisions. This involves gathering data on factors such as market size, customer demographics, competition, regulatory requirements, and cultural considerations.

One key aspect of market research is identifying your target audience in the new market. This involves understanding the needs, preferences, and behavior of potential customers, and tailoring your products or services to meet those needs. You may also need to adapt your marketing and messaging to resonate with the local culture and language.

Another important element of market research is analyzing the competitive landscape in the new market. This includes identifying existing competitors, their strengths and weaknesses, and the unique value proposition that you can offer to stand out in the market. You may also need to assess the regulatory environment and any legal requirements for doing business in the new market.

Market research and analysis are critical for minimizing risk and maximizing the potential for success when expanding into new markets. It provides valuable insights that can inform your strategy and help you make more informed decisions.

5.3 Developing market entry strategies

When expanding into new markets, it's important to have a well-thought-out strategy in place. This includes determining the best approach to enter the market, whether it be through direct investment, strategic partnerships, licensing, or other methods.

In order to develop a successful market entry strategy, businesses must conduct thorough research and analysis of the new market. This includes identifying the target audience, consumer behaviors, cultural nuances, and any legal or regulatory requirements.

One common approach is to adapt existing products or services to the new market, tailoring them to fit the unique needs and preferences of local customers. Alternatively, businesses may choose to develop new products or services specifically for the new market.

Another important consideration when developing market entry strategies is the competitive landscape. It's important to understand the key players in the market, their strengths and weaknesses, and any potential barriers to entry. This information can help businesses differentiate themselves and carve out a niche in the new market.

Developing a solid market entry strategy requires careful planning, research, and analysis to ensure success in the new market.

5.4 Building partnerships and alliances

Expanding into new markets requires a lot of effort, resources, and strategic planning. One way to maximize the chances of success is to form partnerships and alliances with other companies in the market. By building relationships with other businesses, you can leverage their resources, expertise, and customer base to your advantage.

Here are some tips on building partnerships and alliances:

Identify potential partners:

Start by identifying businesses that have a similar target market or complementary products/services. Look for businesses that are well-established in the market and have a good reputation.

Evaluate potential partners:

Once you have identified potential partners, evaluate their strengths and weaknesses. Look for businesses that have complementary strengths to your own and that can add value to your operations.

Develop a partnership strategy:

Once you have identified potential partners, develop a partnership strategy that outlines the goals, objectives, and expectations of the partnership. This will help ensure that both parties are aligned in their approach and that the partnership is beneficial for both parties.

Build relationships:

Once you have developed a partnership strategy, focus on building relationships with your partners. This involves regular communication, mutual respect, and a willingness to collaborate and share ideas.

Monitor and evaluate the partnership:

As with any business relationship, it is important to monitor and evaluate the partnership regularly. This will help ensure that the partnership is meeting its goals and that both parties are benefitting from the relationship.

Overall, building partnerships and alliances is an effective way to expand into new markets and grow your business. By leveraging the strengths of other businesses, you can increase your chances of success and achieve your growth objectives.

Chapter 6: Managing Growth and Change

Chapter 6 focuses on managing the challenges that come with growth and change, including the need to adapt your business processes and structure to accommodate new demands. This chapter will explore strategies for successfully managing growth, including identifying potential roadblocks and taking proactive steps to overcome them. It will also delve into best practices for effectively managing change within your organization, including communicating with stakeholders and ensuring that everyone is on board with the new direction.

6.1 Managing risk and uncertainty

As a business grows and expands, it becomes exposed to new risks and uncertainties that can threaten its success. These risks can come in many forms, such as changes in the economy, new competition, shifting consumer preferences, and disruptive technologies. To manage these risks effectively, businesses need to develop risk management strategies that address potential threats before they arise.

One effective approach is to conduct a risk assessment that identifies the specific risks the business faces and their potential impact on the organization. This can involve analyzing the business environment, conducting scenario planning, and reviewing past experiences to identify patterns and trends.

Once risks have been identified, businesses can develop strategies to mitigate or eliminate them. These strategies might include developing contingency plans, investing in new technologies, or diversifying the business to spread risk.

In addition to managing risks, businesses also need to be able to adapt to change as they grow. This might involve developing new processes and systems, revising business plans, and adopting new technologies. Change management strategies can help businesses navigate these transitions by setting clear goals, communicating effectively with stakeholders, and providing the necessary resources and support to help employees adjust to new ways of working.

Effective risk management and change management are critical to managing growth and ensuring long-term success for businesses of all sizes.

6.2 Adapting to changing market conditions

Adapting to changing market conditions is a critical aspect of managing growth and change for businesses. Markets are dynamic and constantly evolving, and businesses must be able to adapt their strategies to stay competitive and relevant.

One way to adapt to changing market conditions is to stay informed about industry trends and shifts in consumer behavior. This requires ongoing market research and analysis to identify emerging opportunities and threats. It also involves monitoring the activities of competitors and staying up-to-date on advancements in technology and other factors that may impact the market.

Another key aspect of adapting to changing market conditions is having a flexible and agile organizational structure. This means being able to pivot quickly and make strategic decisions in response to market shifts. It may also involve restructuring teams or processes to better align with changing market demands.

Businesses must also be willing to experiment and take calculated risks to remain competitive. This could involve testing new product ideas or entering into new markets to diversify revenue streams. However, it's important to balance these experiments with a solid understanding of the potential risks and rewards.

The ability to adapt to changing market conditions requires a willingness to be proactive and nimble, as well as a strong sense of strategic direction and purpose. By staying attuned to market trends and shifts, and being willing to adjust their strategies and operations accordingly, businesses can better manage growth and change over the long term.

6.3 Building a culture of innovation and creativity

Building a culture of innovation and creativity is critical for managing growth and change in a business. It involves creating an environment where employees are encouraged to think creatively and come up with new ideas and solutions to problems. This can help a business stay ahead of the competition and adapt to changing market conditions.

One way to foster a culture of innovation is to encourage collaboration and teamwork among employees. By bringing together people from different backgrounds and with different skill sets, businesses can create a more diverse and creative workforce. Another way to promote innovation is to provide employees with the resources and support they need to experiment and try new things. This could include access to training, technology, and funding for research and development.

Businesses can also encourage creativity by celebrating and rewarding innovation. This could involve recognizing employees who come up with new ideas or implementing a system for rewarding employees who contribute to the success of the business.

It's important for businesses to create a culture where failure is seen as an opportunity for learning and growth rather than something to be punished or avoided. By encouraging employees to take risks and try new things, businesses can create a more innovative and adaptable culture that is better equipped to manage growth and change.

6.4 Navigating the challenges of rapid growth

Rapid growth can be exciting for a business, but it also comes with its own set of challenges. As a company expands, it must find ways to manage the increased demand for its products or services, while also ensuring that it maintains its standards for quality and customer service.

One of the key challenges of rapid growth is managing cash flow. As a business grows, it may need to invest in new equipment, hire additional employees, or expand its marketing efforts. These investments can be expensive, and it may take time for the company to see a return on its investment. In the meantime, the business may experience cash flow shortages, which can impact its ability to operate effectively.

Another challenge of rapid growth is maintaining the company's culture and values. As a business expands, it may hire new employees who have different backgrounds and experiences. While this can bring fresh perspectives and ideas, it can also create challenges in terms of maintaining the company's culture and values. It's important for businesses to be intentional about preserving their culture as they grow and to communicate their values clearly to new employees.

Rapid growth can put a strain on a company's leadership team. As the business expands, leaders may need to delegate more responsibilities to others and may need to develop new skills in order to manage the growing organization effectively. It's important for leaders to be willing to adapt and to seek out the support they need in order to manage the challenges of rapid growth.

Chapter 7: Financing Growth

Chapter 7 focuses on the critical role of financing in supporting business growth. Even the most promising and well-planned growth strategies require significant investment to execute, which can be a major challenge for many businesses. This chapter explores various sources of funding, from traditional bank loans and venture capital to crowdfunding and government grants. Additionally, it provides guidance on how to identify the right financing options for your business, build a strong case for investment, and manage the risks associated with borrowing and equity financing.

7.1 Understanding the different sources of funding

One of the biggest challenges businesses face when pursuing growth is securing the necessary funding to support expansion efforts. There are many different sources of funding available to businesses, and it's important to understand the advantages and disadvantages of each option in order to make informed decisions about which ones are the best fit for your organization.

Some common sources of funding for growth include bank loans, lines of credit, venture capital, angel investors, crowdfunding, and grants. Each of these options has different requirements, costs, and risks associated with them. For example, bank loans may require collateral and a solid credit history, while venture capital often requires giving up equity in the company. It's important to carefully consider the trade-offs of each option and choose the ones that align with your growth goals and financial situation.

In addition to understanding the different sources of funding, it's also important to understand how to effectively manage and leverage the capital you receive. This may involve creating a detailed financial plan, tracking expenses and revenue, and implementing strategies to maximize profitability and ROI. By taking a strategic and informed approach to financing growth, businesses can position themselves for success and mitigate financial risks along the way.

7.2 Developing a financing strategy

Developing a financing strategy is an essential component of any business's growth plan. A financing strategy involves identifying the various sources of funding available and determining which ones are best suited to meet the business's needs. This requires a thorough understanding of the business's financial requirements, including the amount of capital needed, the timeline for funding, and the expected return on investment.

When developing a financing strategy, it is important to consider the various types of funding available, including debt financing, equity financing, and alternative financing options such as crowdfunding or peer-to-peer lending. Each type of financing has its own advantages and disadvantages, and it is important to evaluate each option carefully to determine which one is the best fit for the business's needs.

Another key consideration when developing a financing strategy is the cost of capital. Different types of funding carry different costs, including interest rates, fees, and equity stakes. It is important to evaluate the cost of each funding option and to determine how it will impact the business's bottom line.

A well-designed financing strategy can help a business achieve its growth objectives by providing the necessary capital to invest in new opportunities and expand operations. By carefully evaluating the available funding options and developing a comprehensive financing plan, businesses can position themselves for long-term success and sustained growth.

7.3 Pitching to investors and securing funding

Once a financing strategy has been developed, the next step is to pitch to potential investors and secure funding. This process requires a clear and compelling pitch that effectively communicates the business's growth potential and how the investor's funds will be used to achieve that growth.

A well-crafted pitch typically includes a concise summary of the business, a clear explanation of the growth opportunity, and a detailed financial plan that demonstrates the potential return on investment. It's important to tailor the pitch to the specific investor or group of investors being targeted, taking into consideration their interests, priorities, and investment criteria.

In addition to traditional funding sources like venture capitalists and angel investors, there are also alternative financing options such as crowdfunding, peer-to-peer lending, and revenue-based financing. Each option has its own pros and cons, so it's important to carefully evaluate which is the best fit for the business's needs and goals.

Once a funding source has been secured, it's important to establish clear expectations and communication with investors, and to diligently manage the business's finances to ensure a healthy return on investment.

7.4 Managing cash flow and financial risks

managing cash flow and financial risks is crucial for any business that wants to grow sustainably. As a company expands, it will likely require more working capital to support its operations and investments. This can put a strain on cash reserves and increase the risk of financial problems.

One way to manage cash flow is by creating a detailed cash flow forecast, which predicts the expected cash inflows and outflows over a given period. This can help a business plan its cash requirements and identify potential cash shortfalls in advance.

Another key aspect of managing financial risks is to maintain adequate financial controls and reporting. This includes regularly reviewing financial statements, identifying and addressing any areas of financial weakness, and establishing clear financial policies and procedures.

Businesses should consider using various financial instruments to manage their financial risks, such as hedging against currency fluctuations, using insurance to manage operational risks, and using derivatives to manage interest rate risks.

By effectively managing cash flow and financial risks, businesses can ensure that they have the necessary funds to fuel their growth and avoid financial problems that could undermine their future success.

Chapter 8: Hiring and Developing a High-Performance Team

 In Chapter 8, we will focus on one of the most important aspects of a successful business - building and maintaining a high-performing team. As your business grows, so too will your need for talented individuals who can help drive your company forward. In this chapter, we'll explore the key principles of team building, from attracting and hiring the right people to developing a culture that fosters innovation and collaboration. We'll also discuss strategies for motivating and retaining your team members, as well as common pitfalls to avoid when building a high-performance team. Whether you're a startup founder or a seasoned business leader, this chapter will provide valuable insights into how to build a winning team that can help take your business to the next level.

8.1 Building a strong company culture

Building a strong company culture is critical for attracting and retaining top talent. A company's culture includes its values, mission, and overall work environment. It can impact how employees interact with each other, their level of job satisfaction, and ultimately, their performance. Companies with a strong culture tend to have employees who are more engaged, motivated, and committed to their work.

To build a strong company culture, business leaders should focus on defining their values and mission, and communicating them effectively to employees. They should also create a positive work environment that promotes collaboration, open communication, and mutual respect. This can be achieved by providing opportunities for team-building, investing in employee development and training, and recognizing and rewarding top performers. A strong company culture can also help attract the right talent and reduce turnover, ultimately leading to increased productivity and profitability.

8.2 Recruiting and hiring top talent

Recruiting and hiring top talent is essential for building a high-performance team that can drive business growth. This involves identifying the skills, experience, and personality traits that are critical for success in each role and then sourcing and evaluating candidates who meet those requirements.

To attract top talent, it's important to have a strong employer brand and an engaging job description that highlights the company's mission, values, and culture. Utilizing various recruitment channels, such as social media, job boards, and employee referrals, can also help to reach a diverse pool of qualified candidates.

Once candidates are identified, a thorough and effective interview process is crucial to assess their fit with the role and the company culture. This may include multiple rounds of interviews with different stakeholders and assessments such as skills tests or case studies.

The goal is to select the best candidate for the role and the company, who has the potential to not only perform the job duties but also to contribute to the company's growth and success in the long term.

8.3 Developing and retaining employees

Developing and retaining employees is crucial to building and maintaining a high-performance team. Once you've recruited top talent, it's important to provide them with opportunities for growth and development within the company. This can include offering training and development programs, mentoring and coaching, and providing regular feedback and performance evaluations.

Another important aspect of retaining employees is creating a positive work environment where employees feel valued and supported. This includes providing competitive compensation and benefits packages, recognizing and rewarding employee achievements, and fostering a culture of open communication and collaboration.

Investing in your employees can have numerous benefits for your business, including increased employee satisfaction and engagement, improved productivity and performance, and reduced turnover rates. By prioritizing employee development and retention, you can build a strong and loyal team that is committed to helping your business achieve its growth goals.

8.4 Building effective teams and leadership

Building effective teams and leadership is a critical component of hiring and developing a high-performance team. Once you have hired top talent and established a strong company culture, it's important to focus on building effective teams and leadership to ensure that your team is working together seamlessly towards achieving common goals.

To build effective teams, it's important to create clear roles and responsibilities for team members and ensure that there is open communication and collaboration among team members. This can be achieved through team-building exercises and regular check-ins to ensure that everyone is on the same page.

In terms of leadership, it's important to have a strong leadership team in place that can provide guidance and support to team members. This includes setting clear expectations for performance and providing regular feedback and coaching to help team members develop their skills and improve their performance.

It's important to foster a culture of continuous learning and development within your organization. This can involve providing training and development opportunities to help employees grow and develop their skills, as well as creating a supportive environment that encourages employees to take on new challenges and try new things.

By building effective teams and leadership, you can create a high-performance culture within your organization that drives success and growth.

Chapter 9: Scaling and Growth for the Future

In Chapter 9, we will explore the long-term considerations for scaling and growth in your business. It is important to have a vision for the future and a plan to achieve that vision. This chapter will cover topics such as creating a sustainable business model, embracing innovation and new technologies, expanding globally, and developing a long-term strategy for growth. By understanding these concepts and implementing them effectively, your business can achieve long-term success and continued growth in the future.

9.1 Preparing for future growth opportunities

Preparing for future growth opportunities is an essential aspect of scaling and growth for the future. In this chapter, you will learn about the importance of thinking ahead and identifying potential growth areas for your business. By anticipating future opportunities, you can position your business to take advantage of them when they arise.

One way to prepare for future growth opportunities is by staying up-to-date with industry trends and emerging technologies. This involves keeping an eye on the latest developments in your industry, attending conferences and networking events, and connecting with thought leaders and experts in your field. By doing so, you can identify new areas of growth and innovation that may be relevant to your business.

Another important aspect of preparing for future growth is developing a flexible and adaptable business strategy. This means being willing to pivot or adjust your approach as needed to respond to changing market conditions or emerging opportunities. By having a clear understanding of your business goals and objectives, you can make strategic decisions that will help you scale and grow in the future.

9.2 Leveraging technology and innovation

In today's fast-paced and technologically advanced world, leveraging technology and innovation has become a critical aspect of scaling and growing a business. By adopting new technologies and innovative strategies, companies can streamline their operations, enhance their products or services, and better meet the changing needs of their customers.

One key aspect of leveraging technology and innovation is to stay up to date with the latest trends and advancements in your industry. This means investing in research and development, attending industry events and conferences, and networking with other professionals in your field. Another important aspect is to embrace new technologies and tools that can improve your business operations. This may include implementing new software systems, adopting automation tools, or exploring the use of artificial intelligence (AI) and machine learning (ML) to analyze data and make more informed decisions.

Innovation is also crucial for staying ahead of the competition and anticipating future trends. This means encouraging creative thinking and experimentation within your team, and being open to new ideas and approaches to solving problems.

By leveraging technology and innovation, businesses can not only achieve short-term growth and success, but also position themselves for long-term sustainability and competitiveness in their industry.

9.3 Embracing sustainability and social responsibility

 As businesses grow and expand, they also have a responsibility to ensure their operations are sustainable and socially responsible. This includes reducing their impact on the environment, investing in renewable energy, implementing ethical business practices, and supporting social causes.

Leveraging technology and innovation can play a significant role in achieving sustainability goals. For example, companies can adopt digital technologies to streamline their operations and reduce paper waste. They can also explore the use of renewable energy sources such as solar and wind power, or invest in energy-efficient technologies.

Additionally, companies can embrace sustainability by designing products and services that have a minimal impact on the environment. For example, they can use eco-friendly materials, reduce packaging waste, or develop products that can be recycled or reused.

Social responsibility is also an important consideration for businesses. They can support social causes by partnering with non-profit organizations or launching their own corporate social responsibility (CSR) initiatives. This can include supporting local communities, investing in education and training programs, or donating a portion of their profits to charitable causes.

Embracing sustainability and social responsibility is not only good for the environment and society, but it can also be a key driver of business success and growth in the long run.

9.4 Continuously learning and evolving

Continuous learning and evolution are key elements of scaling and growth for the future. As a business grows and expands, it must continue to adapt to new market trends, customer needs, and technological advancements. This requires a commitment to ongoing learning and development for both the organization as a whole and its individual employees.

One way to foster continuous learning is through regular training and development programs. This can include workshops, seminars, and online courses to help employees stay up-to-date on the latest industry trends and best practices. Employers can also encourage their teams to attend conferences and networking events to gain new insights and ideas.

Businesses should prioritize a culture of innovation and experimentation. This means creating an environment where employees feel encouraged to try new things, take risks, and learn from both successes and failures. By fostering a culture of innovation, businesses can stay agile and adaptable, even as they grow and expand.

Another important aspect of scaling and growth for the future is a commitment to sustainability and social responsibility. This means taking steps to reduce the environmental impact of the business, while also supporting the needs of the communities in which it operates. This can include initiatives like reducing waste and emissions, supporting local suppliers and vendors, and promoting diversity and inclusion within the organization.

Businesses that prioritize continuous learning, innovation, and sustainability are more likely to succeed in the long term. By embracing change and evolution, they can stay ahead of the curve and continue to grow and thrive, even in the face of new challenges and opportunities.

Conclusion

In conclusion, scaling and growing a business is a complex and challenging process that requires a clear strategy, effective management, and continuous innovation. This book has provided an overview of the key concepts, strategies, and best practices for successfully scaling a business.

To begin, it is essential to define the goals and objectives of the growth strategy, identify key initiatives and action plans, assign responsibilities, and monitor progress. It is crucial to streamline processes and workflows, automate tasks and functions, outsource and delegate responsibilities, and manage resources effectively. Moreover, expanding into new markets requires identifying new opportunities, conducting market research and analysis, developing market entry strategies, and building partnerships and alliances.

Managing growth and change requires managing risk and uncertainty, adapting to changing market conditions, building a culture of innovation and creativity, and navigating the challenges of rapid growth. Financing growth requires understanding the different sources of funding, developing a financing strategy, pitching to investors and securing funding, and managing cash flow and financial risks.

Hiring and developing a high-performance team is crucial for scaling a business. This requires building a strong company culture, recruiting and hiring top talent, developing and retaining employees, and building effective teams and leadership. Finally, scaling and growth for the future requires preparing for future growth opportunities, leveraging technology and innovation, embracing sustainability and social responsibility, and continuously learning and evolving.

In today's dynamic business environment, businesses must continually adapt and innovate to remain competitive and relevant. The principles outlined in this book provide a framework for scaling and growing a business while maintaining a focus on sustainable growth and long-term success.

It is important to note that there is no one-size-fits-all approach to scaling a business. Each business is unique, and the growth strategy must be tailored to the specific needs and challenges of the business. Moreover, scaling and growth require a significant investment of time, resources, and capital. Businesses must be prepared to make these investments and be willing to take calculated risks to achieve their growth objectives.

In conclusion, scaling and growing a business can be a challenging and rewarding process. With the right strategy, effective management, and continuous innovation, businesses can achieve sustainable growth and long-term success. This book has provided a comprehensive overview of the key concepts, strategies, and best practices for successfully scaling a business. It is now up to businesses to implement these principles and take action towards achieving their growth objectives.